A Journey in Suicide

Coping After The Suicide Of A Loved One

By

TERESA MULERO O'BRIEN

Dedications

Introduction

In the first instant I discovered my husband, my first thought was, "No." *"Where are you?" "Where is your soul?" "Where did you go?"* I started to cry deep sobs. "You're not here anymore, so where are you?" I began to shake as the burning in my chest intensified. I was scared, and it felt freaky to have seen this. *How could he leave us? Were we really that bad? Why? How am I supposed to live without you here in this world?* I felt so alone already; how was I going to tell my kids, now grown up. One married with one son and one on the way in two months and having his name as the middle name. How were we going to tell our grandchild where his poppy went? Life will never be the same, and it wasn't.

Table of Contents

Chapter 1

The Stillness and the Numb

In the hours leading up to my discovery; the morning began as a cold Sunday six days before Christmas in 2016. The tree was up, adorned with old ornaments from every year of our children's lives to before we were married, along with present-day grandchild and grandchild on the way. Gifts were bought, wrapped and stocked well up on the top floor spare room. My parents had just left, having had their ritualistic coffee on Sunday morning as they always did. Everything was as it should be.

No signs of anything strange or out of the ordinary. But out of nowhere, an argument broke out about a mini car table my son had bought our grandson for Christmas. We thought it would have been a good idea to keep it here in the dining room so he could play with it when he came here.

My daughter had a small apartment and didn't want to overcrowd it. My husband disagreed and thought it should go to their house. The opinions escalated.

My parents went home, and we were left arguing. My husband became enraged that he was being challenged. We couldn't believe he was being so ridiculously negative about a toy. The more we tried to reason with him, the angrier he got. As a matter of fact, I had never seen him angrier about something in a long while. Lots of words were exchanged, and some I'd like to forget that were said. We stood up to him because it was something that we agreed should never have been a big deal in the first place. He began to behave violently, and I grabbed my son and led us to the bedroom, where I locked the door behind us.

We all went our separate ways that day and came back later. We were just giving him a chance to cool down. When I walked back into the house, I saw a stillness that I can't describe. I have never experienced it before and have not since.

Something wasn't right. My dog was acting nervous, walking all over the house and following me. Afterward, I remember thinking he must have sensed something. They say dogs know when a soul leaves. As far as I knew, my husband was still in the basement office. I didn't want to bother him or fight more. I was giving it the proper time to pass, as all things do. I went to bed, figuring he'd come up eventually. He never did again.

I woke up at 4 am to his alarm clock ringing and he wasn't in bed. I got up, and I looked for him in every room. Everything was still and quiet. My dog followed. I opened the basement door and walked down the stairs. My dog didn't follow. He stayed up at the top of the steps. I thought that was odd. I went to the office room, and he wasn't there. He wasn't on the couch in the main basement area either. I went into the boiler room, and through the narrow space of the heater, I saw his shoes about two feet off the floor.

My heart skipped beats and pounded fast; I couldn't believe what I saw. I covered my eyes and my mouth from letting out a scream. I gathered myself and went around the heater to where he was. He had a black trash bag over his head. I took the bag off his head. I don't know why I did this; maybe I was in disbelief, hoping it was not him. I saw those sneakers, and I knew it was. I couldn't move; I didn't want to believe it and see him like this. I began to cry, but I was stiff as a board. I stepped back, and my life flashed before my eyes. *What will I do without you?*

I ran up the stairs and into my mom's apartment, where I knocked on the door frantically. I was trying to tell her, but the words were not coming out of my mouth. I finally did, and she began saying, *"No, no, why?"* Then my son came in.

I guess he heard my knocking, and I could barely tell him;
I did, and he fell to pieces. We still had to tell my seven-
month- pregnant daughter and her husband. This was
going to be the hardest day of my life.

It was. To this very day, it still is.

Chapter 2

First Glance

I never thought this was in the works. There had been worse times before. We had tried to get Ray's help, but he was stubborn and refused. My son and I begged him to consider it. He told us to *"stop making mistakes,"* and he won't need to get upset. I knew he was bipolar—just a good guess from my education as a medical assistant for 21 years. I can basically say I have seen a lot in my career.

The conversation took place two years before this tragedy. To him, the answer was no, just that! My son and I felt a mutual sadness. We knew then that he would never change. He continued with the same wild temper he had had for years. There were days when he was completely normal, loving, and caring.

This was truly who he was. This is how I base it on being bipolar. When you pretty much don't know what mood you are going to get at any given moment, that's when you can safely assume it's bipolar. I had been living with this man for 32 years. We were together since we were 17 and 18 years old. We were now together longer than we had both lived with our parents. We were engraved into each other. When he was loving, he loved better than anyone. When he was nasty, he was the worst I had ever seen.

I was married to him, and we had a life and children. I was an old-fashioned, devoted wife, just as my mother had been to my father. It was the only way I knew how to live, and I believed in it. You could say I was a devout Catholic and believed in the promises we made before God to each other. I believed I could keep my family intact. I was always trying to make things better for him and my kids. For everyone who lived in my house, I tried to make it all work. I did not want my kids to be latchkey kids, growing up with parents who were always gone and working. I wanted to be there for them.

So, when they walked into the house after school, they were greeted by me or it was me who picked them up safely from school. I wanted to take them to their sports or Activities. I worked around their schedule. To others, this may not have made sense, but for me, it was the only way I knew. I didn't want to be divorced, and I didn't want my kids to be in a broken home. I wanted to win this for them, for me, and for their dad. He was all I knew. Ray worked hard. He worked in a worldwide company for 30 years, since he was 18 years old, and climbed up the corporate ladder.

He was a devoted employee and loved his job. But he really started to feel pinched and tired. They put a lot of pressure on him, always giving him new projects they wouldn't give anyone else. He never called in sick. That last year, he Did the most, and I noticed it. I tried to talk to him about it. He said he wished there was Another buy-out in the works. This is when they'd offer a hefty severance pay for you to step out quietly. We would have been well off till his retirement. He said he would have accepted It. Turns out that wasn't in the works. They needed him very much. That's how much of a difference he made in that company. His frustration grew. I tried to tell him many times throughout our lives together that he needed to take meds to be grounded. He would deny that right away and say he wasn't going on anything.

He had tried Prozac 10 years before when the kids were little. To this day, we remember how calm and happy he was while he was on it. It made such a big difference. However, moving to New Jersey seemed to be the downfall. Upon meeting his new doctor, he was told that his blood pressure was elevated, probably due to the Prozac. They didn't speak any further about it. Ray just decided to go off it. He was health conscious and didn't want any problems from it that would affect his health. This was where it all started. Every day from then on, he was different. He could walk out of the house in a great mood and walk back in a half hour later and slam that door so hard that the house shook.

The kids were about teens by now. The teens and Ray did not mix well, and he was having a hard time seeing his kids growing up. He was very strict with them. It was hard on them and everyone else in the home, including my parents. He'd be embarrassing and condescending at times. I did the best I could to be the buffer. But that wore me down.

Chapter 3

Steps to Realism

I went through many stages after my loss. One of which I had the hardest time with was the realization that this really did happen. He really killed himself. My days seemed cloudy and surreal. I felt like I was trapped in a gray fog that I could not get out of. My days did not look or feel the same at all. There was not that old comfortable feeling people mostly felt by being in their own house. I felt ungrounded. I did not know where I belonged anymore. I couldn't realize that my world, how I knew it, had changed, and I had to change with it. I was stuck in my past, and my house was so full of my husband. Full of his footsteps, the clinking of glasses, his sounds, coffee being made, his favorite show on TV, his laughter, his yelling…everything. I felt like he was still there. I just couldn't see him. It was quiet in the house now, like a cold loneliness. He should have been here, but he wasn't. I felt like I should not be there either. After days of feeling like this and not being able to sleep in my bed since he left, I decided I had to create new routines. Either that or I'd die with him. That wasn't me. I wouldn't cause pain for anyone else, even if it would end mine. I chose life. Why? Well, I had kids who loved me and a grandchild who loved me, and I loved them. I wanted to be here. Even though I was lost, I needed to be here. I needed to meet my new grandchild and sit with the one I had. Ray had already let them down, and I couldn't. Of all the things I didn't know, being a fighter was one of them. My son, who lived with me, literally picked me off the floor one day because I just broke down and sobbed. I just didn't know how I was going to get through this. He held me close, told me he loved me, and said, "You can do this, Mom." Even if I couldn't for me, I knew I could for him because he believed in me.

The more I made new days for myself, planning, keeping busy, and getting back to work after three months, the more things began to fall into place. A new place. I would never have believed it if someone had told me that I had to go through the motions until it became my life, my new life! I didn't know how it would be and where it would lead, but I had two kids and two grandkids. And I had to see what the future would hold, come what may. It is not an easy road, but it is the right one. Dying is hard; living is harder.

Chapter 4

Pain

Despite my newfound promises, my body wasn't going to let me get away with not experiencing Physical pain in my loss. Yes, your body feels physical trauma in response to the mental trauma. I was not ready for this. It happened the first night I slept back in my bed alone since Ray had Left. I had a hard time sleeping without him.

It was so hard sleeping without that same person next to me, like I did for the past 32 years of my life. I would wake up in the morning, open my eyes and reality would hit me all over again. I experienced a searing physical pain in the middle of my chest. I would cry out. My son would run into the room and try to comfort me. I would just think, *"When will this ever stop?"* Here I was, trying my best to put my life back together, and I was left to realize every morning, like a shock, as if it was happening again for the first time, like those first moments with the pain of my loss. I often thought, *"So, is this what I'm left with"*? I knew this had to get better, but I had no idea how long it would take. I just had to go with it.

Until one day, I'd wake up, and it wouldn't jolt me out of bed. Maybe I'd wake up and just open my eyes and feel the peace of a new day. Eventually, it did happen. It seemed like forever. When it did, I didn't open my eyes. I just lay there enjoying the fact that I was there, I was safe, and I was not in physical pain. In that stillness, a new reality began to take shape. It was called survival. It was still hard, but it did not hurt as much.

Chapter 5

Finding your place in an empty space

I didn't know where I belonged anymore. I felt displaced. My mind was quiet, filled with a kind of white noise. During those days, I felt like I was always a minute away from falling apart. I became clingy with my son. At one point, I needed him to sit with me in the living room because I couldn't stand being alone. Being in a room alone was too much for me. I felt lost and was very unnatural. I knew I needed a reason and a way to push through all this. I needed to let my son find his own way in this, too, and come out whole again. Smothering him was not the answer. I needed to get up on two feet and live my life, at least learn how to. I felt it was God's purpose for me. I had codependent tendencies, so for someone like that, this becomes doubly hard. During this time, I started attending grief counseling and suicide counseling, which is much different. I learned how many problems could be resolved through forgiveness.

When a person commits suicide, their suffering ends, but for us, it's just the beginning. It just passes it over to whoever is left grieving.

I had to sit and talk to my beloved and express how I felt. I also needed to tell him that I forgave him. It wasn't going to help me go on and be well enough to hold on to the anger and the pain, so I sat one time in the exact place he last was. I said I forgave him, but I wished he could have reached out to a friend, called a family meeting, or just gone to sleep; anything but what he did? But he was too far gone. The guilt I felt was overwhelming, almost unconscionable. I cried so much, deep sobs of cries from the middle of my chest, that I started to look twice my age. I wish he had seen a friend when he went to Lowe's to buy the rope. I wish, I wish, I wish.

Chapter 6

Getting to Know the World Again

The one thing that truly needed to happen was learning to exist with myself. I'm not going to stay alone because we are never truly alone. God is your partner in life. This new beginning surrounded me and my inner strength. I soon came to find out that the only way for me to survive this loss was to look at it as a new beginning. Although my husband chose to leave, this was a new beginning for him as well. *"What have I not done that I'd like to do?"* I asked myself. *"What can I do by myself to begin again?"* So, I made a bucket list. I made a list of everything I ever wanted to do, including writing this book. I have done most of what was on that list. There are a couple of things I'm still working on. I thought of all I was doing at the time at my home, all by myself. I remember thinking, *"Boy, would he be proud of me."* I smiled to myself, but I knew I must keep moving through the fog. I never felt that way about myself before, but I was proud of myself. For the first time, I began to feel like I could survive. I was doing the bills by myself, deciding about what I wanted to eat for dinner. I had my son there, but he was easy. Should I continue to live here, or should I move?

Ultimately, I decided to stay and pay off my mortgage with the money Ray had left for me. I did this so everyone could stay put. No one had to upheaval themselves to find a better situation. This, for that time, worked out perfectly. I made that decision with a little help from my dad, who suggested it; I had never thought of doing that. Besides, it gave me comfort to stay where we brought up our children, where my grandchildren played, and where the memories we made were all around. I needed those memories and I was not ready to put them in a box. Ray was here, and he made a difference. He was wrong in doing what he did to himself and us, but we still loved him more than ever. I wanted to keep his memory alive. I want to say his name and joke about the silly things we laughed at. Those are the very things that help you heal. There would still be crying at times, but we were comforted by our home where he lived and died.

Chapter 7

Helpless to "I got this"!

I didn't know what to do without Ray. I had been with him longer than I was on my own and with my parents. He was a bit of a control freak, so he had to do everything with the bills and money in our home. I did what I had to do with my little paycheck, which was relatively simple. It was my job to pay my son's college tuition and get my nails done every two weeks.

Other than that, he paid the bills and was meticulous about it. I had no trouble following his lead when it came to making the payments. But now, there were books and copies of important papers all over; I felt so overwhelmed. I had no idea how I was going to get through all of this, but I knew I needed to. My brother and a couple of family friends tried to help, but if I didn't know where certain things were, how could they? I felt lost in this chaotic paperwork and responsibilities.

After the first couple of weeks, when things quieted down a bit, I sat with it all laid across my kitchen table. One by one, I sorted things out. I made a ton of phone calls, creating a pending file, a call file, and a finished file. Slowly but surely, I was getting things done. The table was clearing. It took me weeks, and I longed for someone to come and do it for me so I could just grieve. I felt like I had no time to grieve. I had to put my life back together. This step couldn't be brushed aside. It had to be done.

Once everything was done, I felt like I could live my life more calmly. I felt like I could do it myself. This made me stronger and more confident. I felt less lost.

Bank statements, bills, 401(k), and life insurance policies are not what you want to deal with after the loss of someone you love. People from those establishments will call and must ask questions, need numbers, and ask for information.

I faced tough decisions about whether to return cars or pay them off to maintain a household and live within my means. I was never the sole breadwinner in our house, so I had to decide about keeping the home or selling it. I wanted to make smart decisions to accommodate all of us: my son and I, my parents, a dog, and a cat. So, I put my house up for sale.

But as I searched for a new property, nothing seemed right for all of us. I saw that nothing was better than what we had. My dad suggested that I should pay it off with the insurance money left for me. I consulted my lawyer, and he said it sounded like the best decision for me. That is just what I did.

After that, we were able to breathe a sigh of relief. I never wanted to be alone. I wanted it to be Ray and I until we got old and passed on. This was not my choice. So, I did the best I could without him. I needed to be my own boss and make all the decisions now. God had other plans. Now, it was just me.

Chapter 8

Where do I go from here?

I would say that anger and sadness do linger the longest. Now that I had to go and do "me" and get myself moving on again, I decided to do things a bit differently. This way was not going to make others happy. By others, I mean my parents, children, and close friends. I suspected they may have wanted to see me in the suffering mode a little bit before I tried to move on from it. I don't at all mean anything bad by this or against them. Everyone has a picture of what grieving should look like.

I played that part for months, but it did not serve me well. I needed to get out of that realm. It just wasn't working out too well. Reality was becoming a problem. I felt alone for years—especially in my relationship. As my husband withdrew socially, I became more isolated and lonely. I was that way for a while. I wanted to see if I could love someone else and if there could be a male/female friendship. I was sitting on the couch too long, thinking about what our last conversation was and what he would be doing if he were here. I could have done that forever. I was so tired of feeling like I was going to be stuck there forever. No one was going to do it for me. It was something I had to do for myself.

Going to grief counselors and suicide counseling was not all that life had left for me. There had to be more, and I was going to search for it. I spent 32 years married to Ray and four years dating each other before that. It started in high school. The girls loved him, but I liked him more. I decided to ask him to my senior prom, and he said yes. It was March 10th. The prom was not until May 10th. Would we remain friends, become a couple, or drift apart? We chose to get to know each other, and that's how it all began.

That's how it all began. I considered myself so lucky to know him. To be his friend and to be in his arms. We were inseparable.

Looking back, if I could have foreseen everything that happened, would I still do it all over again? My answer is YES! Knowing Ray was one of the best things to ever happen to me. We had a genuine love for each other. People who choose suicide are not bad people; they are just trapped inside their own heads and cannot find a way to break loose. He gave me two children that I love so much. We went through the hard times together and never gave in. I suspect that the tidal wave in his head just became too much for him to fight. I wish he had fought harder. For all the fighting he did in his life with me and others, making him the argumentative person that he was, I wished he would have screamed louder to break away and scream for help. Nobody knew it was that bad. We tried as much as we could to lead him to peace, but he fought us to the end. I wanted him just to fight himself, not against the people who loved him.

Chapter 9

The Family

Sometimes, with family, you don't find the understanding that you expect. Instead, you find judgment. A lot of people were disappointed that I decided to date sooner than they felt was right. I was ridiculed by someone once but after I heard them say what they said, I thought to myself all the days I sat there and cried day in and day out. At that time, they just wanted me to snap out of it. I was told people lose their husbands every day. I remember responding, *"Not like this, they don't."* I was furious.

This was no ordinary death. This is not an occurrence that happens to everyone one day in their lives. Maybe death does, but not suicide. I wondered to myself, *"Well, which one is it"? Do they want me to mourn, or do they want me to move on?* I decided then that they would talk and judge no matter what I did. They weren't going through it; I was! It's unimaginable that people would have any expectations of me at a time like that. I was just trying to breathe every day. I was just trying to find something left for me in this world.

I felt that once Ray was gone, there wasn't too much of a future for me on planet Earth. I put all my eggs in one basket. That's the way I was, always jumping in with both feet, never thinking, just jumping. Friends came and went.

My husband and my two children were always there for me. I loved it that way. I never wanted more except for the peace I never got. I never really had a life of my own.

I gave that up. I got involved with everything my kids loved: school, sports, dance, gymnastics, drums, bands, cosmetology, and birthday parties. Anything they loved, I was involved in. It gave me pride in them for being their mother. They were my all, my everything. I mean, *"Wasn't that what being a parent is all about?"*

All I had left of my life with Ray were my children, and I treasured them deeply. They were what he gave me, and I gave him them. He was here, and he was real. He lived a life like everybody else. No matter how he chose to die, I would not let the world forget him. He Had a heart of gold. He'd give you the shirt off his back. I know people use that term often, but he literally gave the shoes off his feet to a poor man in Punta Cana, Dominican Republic. I will not let anyone forget that. I did not forget him, and I won't.

To this very day, he is spoken about as if he is still here. Even my current husband feels like he knows him. He understands him for some reason and feels like, in some ways, they are a lot alike. In other ways, they are nothing alike. It takes a special kind of person to understand a man he never met. A man who his wife loved and still does because love just doesn't die with a person. It lives way beyond the years of that lifetime. I love Chris differently; it is a strong love, too. I thank God for the love that exists for me today.

Chapter 10

Signs

I began noticing signs that Ray was still there with me from the very beginning. Just two days after he passed, there were pennies all over my backyard deck. No one was out there. It was cold, holiday time, and we were busy making funeral arrangements. The door was only opened to let the dog out. I thought, *"No, this can't be."* It really does happen. Then, two doves, a couple of days after, flew right into my living room window.

Then, shortly after that, a dove flew into my sliding glass doors leading out to my backyard deck. I was startled because I was standing there just staring out those glass doors, thinking of him. We both had a fascination with the two doves that lived in the tree in my yard. They were always together. Ray took pictures of all the little animals in our yard. He was an avid photographer who had been taking pictures for years of all kinds of things around him. He loved that house and all the little creatures who lived around it. Squirrels, birds, chipmunks, even bees, and certain insects he found interesting. I knew when I saw those doves fly into the glass doors that that was him letting me know he was around. That gave me so much comfort. The day I married Chris, my son, was with me in front of our home, and it was a beautiful, sunny, picture-perfect day in April.

The photographer was taking pictures of us, and the limousine pulled up to the driveway to pick us up and bring us to the church. The driver had the music playing loudly, and suddenly, a song came on that reminded my son and me of Ray. We exchanged glances, and I whispered, *"He's here with us."*

We were astonished that even on a day meant to celebrate new beginnings, Ray's presence was so palpable. Life doesn't end. It just continues on the other side, the eternal side, where we live forever in harmony with our divine creator and the heavenly angels and saints that guide us through our lives. This is how I see it. To this day, I can't see it any other way. It's strange to say and for some people to hear, but I know he loved me so very much. I know he regretted doing what he did. I knew he never meant to hurt us in this way. I forgave him even though I would get angry at him for doing what he did and for putting our family through so much turmoil. It ended for him but would have long-lasting effects on his wife, his kids, and all of us.

Chapter 11

Guilt

From time to time, I would really start to think and wonder what I could have done to change this outcome. I would cry and begin to feel that crushing pain in the middle of my chest again. That hurt so much physically. I would think about all that could have been, and maybe all that should have been. What could I have done differently that day to get a different outcome? Through therapy, I learned that it simply wasn't my call. It wasn't my daughter's call or my son's call either. It was simply his decision. Like it or not, it was what he chose. My son and I had been proactive in urging him to seek help. My daughter was not living at home any longer and did not witness all the struggles we had in the last couple of years. It wasn't her responsibility to save him, just as it wasn't ours.

I know we all felt some guilt. Something we all could agree on, though, was that it was not our life. It was his. I know at times, guilt consumed me.

I was stuck in the rut of trying to think up so many scenarios. I was told the outcome only changes if the person themselves wants that change. It was never enough for us to want it; it was always up to him. It took me many years to realize this. The guilt and sorrow I carried around for years was suffocating me. It was a dark cloud that was on top of me in everything I did, experienced, and felt. The only day that cloud lifted was the day I married Chris. I think that was such a beautiful day that God spared me of this dooming feeling. Sometimes, I even think it was Ray who said, *"Not today"! Today belongs to you and Chris, and I am just here to wish you joy."*

Chapter 12

Opinions

Don't let the fear of opinions coming from people divert you from what you really want in life. Stop trying to get everyone on board and agree with what you are doing. Pray and listen to the signs God gives you. Your decisions may be right for you, but you may not have the blessings of others. It's your path and your life. If the people in your life truly have your best interests at heart, they will love you. Regardless, after going through such trauma, no one should place any holds on you or impose any specific expectations, judgment, or criticism. They have not walked in your shoes or felt your exact same emotions to know what is right and what is wrong. No one does, except you. I encountered such things. Honestly, though, their opinions never bothered me. I was starting to learn to put people where they belonged. What I mean by that is, if they put me last, that is where I learned to put them. Life becomes a big reality check. Judgment comes from people you less expect it from. At first, it shocks you. Then you realize that it's because they have an ulterior motive.

They start to question where they fit in your new life. They don't want to move a notch from where they've been. If they have to, you're in trouble. Attitudes change, and here comes the judgment. I always wanted to know why they should care what you do and what decisions you make as long as you are happy. After what I've been through, who could or should expect anything from me?

I was totally amazed by the judgment I received from people I never expected. I really started to learn how sheltered my life had been. I got judgment on where I was, who I was with, and how long I was gone. I know that they cared, but it was not only for that reason. When I sat around and cried, I was told, *"Life goes on."* When I got up and went, I was told to slow down. My advice is to do what you feel, and it will bring you the happiness that you need to move forward with your life. It has to be how you want it, when you want it, and wherever that may be.

Chapter 13

The Promise to myself

After going through so much and being so tired of the ups and downs of my emotions, I decided I would not consume myself with guilt over anything. This realization came to me about two years after Ray passed.

The guilt that a suicide survivor goes through is more than a soul can handle. I had to let it go. I had to learn that it was not my responsibility to keep Ray alive. It was not my responsibility to be careful of everything and to walk on eggshells with someone's life and mortality. That's why it's called *"Your own life."*

No one can do it for you. If you make mistakes, no one can be held responsible for them, but only you. It was not my decision. I will not mourn a life that was no longer here because he chose it not to be. I miss him, I always will, but I will not get stuck in that rut that traps me. No one told me this, and no one explained any of this to me. It's simply just what I learned; therefore, I am passing it on to you in the hopes that someone such as I can relate to you, what no one will ever tell you.

I needed to find a life that I was comfortable and content with every day. Every day is a gift; it's not a waste. I don't have to move mountains; all I had to do was breathe. To me, that was enough. It's a relief, it's a contentment, and it's a joy. I want to just be and love every minute of every day that is mine and belongs to me. By praying often, God led me to this. Awake or asleep, He has gotten me through my catastrophe.The world didn't have to know; I knew. Now you do, too.

Chapter 14

Oh, the milestones you have missed

From the beginning of his end, I couldn't believe for the longest time how Ray chose to leave. With so much on the horizon. The birth of another grandson who would be his namesake, our son's college graduation, our daughter and son-in-law's first home, and me, the glue that held this little family together for so long, the peacekeeper. These things did not enter his mind, but his mind was taken over by a dreadful emotion that stole his love, laughter, and will to survive. Most of the memories I have of him consist of being nervous and socially shut down. The anger, anxiety, and depression were like a title wave that took over everything. He could never just sit and relax. Even though we had been together for 32 years, he was detached from the happiness he should have felt. That left me feeling isolated. Ray was one of the most gifted people I ever knew in my life. I was always so proud of all the things he could do and accomplish.

He came from nothing, and his determination never faltered, at least not until the end. I realize how hard it is not to want to just give up. After I lost him, I felt like this, and it hurt like hell. The most wonderful thing is how much he was loved. So many people came and gave their respects, an amount I was truly amazed at. If he had only realized the love, respect, and acceptance people had for him, I sincerely feel he would not have chosen to leave. I'm so sorry he was hurting and so sorry for all the pain he felt as a child. It was not his fault. The only wrong thing was the way he chose to deal with it. I understood what his childhood was like. Being alone, a latchkey kid, and being left with people who hurt him and took advantage of him. This is the part he never talked about or got help with. My only wish was that he would have wanted to unburden himself of this and talk and get the help he needed. I accepted him and loved him unconditionally.

Chapter 15

Last Words

For us, Ray and I, there were no last words of goodbye; I'll see you again. I never got to say anything. I guess I can say it now. Thank you, Ray, for giving us, the kids and me, the best life you knew how. Thank you for the love and loyalty you were able to show when you were alive and with us. We had some beautiful moments, and I remember them all.

I chose to hold on over everything else and those horrible last moments of your life. I chose to see the heart inside that tough exterior. I hope wherever you are, you have found your peace. Giving love and forgiveness is what this life is all about. The way God loves and forgives us, we, in turn, must do the same. Through it all, I learned I can do this, and I have.

EPILOGUE

Suicide doesn't end the chances of life getting worse, it eliminates The possibility of it ever getting any better.

Unknown-

Afterward

I hope you can see from this small book that we all have life lessons to learn and go through.

There is lots to learn and always a reason why. It's not what we are given but how we handle it. That is the key.

Faith, love, and forgiveness are really the only answers I could come up with. That is what helps us get through it all: get going and persevere.

It's amazing how some of us miss this. I was once one of them.

Thank you for reading my journey. I hope it helps you with yours.

~ Teresa

ABOUT THE AUTHOR

Teresa Mulero O'Brien is a former medical assistant with 22 years of experience in New York and New Jersey. Recently, she embarked on her journey as a new author, driven by her love of poetry and true stories. This is her first book.

Teresa resides in Conway, South Carolina, with her husband, Chris, and their two dogs, Fizz and Phebee, as well as two cats, Tully and Brandy. She also manages a Facebook page titled "Soul Survivors of Suicide," a supportive space where people can share their stories and find inspiration in what it means to be a survivor.

Currently, Teresa is working on her second book, which she plans to release in the near future.